José Garrido
Kennesaw State University

ALICE
Programming Language

JONES AND BARTLETT PUBLISHERS
Sudbury, Massachusetts
BOSTON TORONTO LONDON SINGAPORE

World Headquarters
Jones and Bartlett Publishers
40 Tall Pine Drive
Sudbury, MA 01776
978-443-5000
info@jbpub.com
www.jbpub.com

Jones and Bartlett Publishers Canada
6339 Ormindale Way
Mississauga, Ontario L5V 1J2
CANADA

Jones and Bartlett Publishers International
Barb House, Barb Mews
London W6 7PA
UK

Jones and Bartlett's books and products are available through most bookstores and online booksellers. To contact Jones and Bartlett Publishers directly, call 800-832-0034, fax 978-443-8000, or visit our website, www.jbpub.com.

Substantial discounts on bulk quantities of Jones and Bartlett's publications are available to corporations, professional associations, and other qualified organizations. For details and specific discount information, contact the special sales department at Jones and Bartlett via the above contact information or send an email to specialsales@jbpub.com.

Production Credits
Acquisitions Editor: Tim Anderson
Production Director: Amy Rose
Editorial Assistant: Laura Pagluica
Production Assistant: Mike Boblitt
Manufacturing Buyer: Therese Connell
Marketing Manager: Andrea DeFronzo
Composition: Northeast Compositors, Inc.
Cover Design: Kristin E. Ohlin
Cover Image: © Tina Rencelj/ShutterStock, Inc.
Printing and Binding: Malloy, Inc.
Cover Printing: Malloy, Inc.

ISBN-13: 978-0-7637-5059-6
ISBN-10: 0-7637-5059-X

6048

Printed in the United States of America
12 11 10 09 08 10 9 8 7 6 5 4 3 2

contents

Introduction

A computer (or computer system) can carry out specific tasks only by following the sequences of instructions, together with data descriptions, found in a program. The computer executes the program by performing one instruction after the other in the specified order and carrying out some computations on the data.

An algorithm is a detailed step-by-step solution to a problem. A program is a computer implementation of an algorithm. Developing a program is an important aspect of problem solving that requires knowledge of a programming language and associated environment. The programs constitute the software components of a computer system. Programming is about the design and construction of programs.

This manual describes the general usage of Alice as a unique system and tool for learning programming, and how to construct programs in Alice. The manual also describes the general principles of modeling with objects. Most of the material explains how to use Alice to define objects in a three-dimensional environment (called a virtual world) and how to dynamically manipulate these objects. The Alice system makes it possible to better understand the introductory notions of programming.

Programming and Languages

A programming language is a formal notation that is used to write the data description and the instructions of a program. The programming language has a well-defined set of syntax and semantic rules. The syntax rules describe how to write sentences; the semantic rules describe the meaning of the sentences. These two types of rules must be consistent.

2.1 Machine Languages

Before the early programming languages were developed, programmers had to use machine languages designed for the various computers. Until the early 1950s, this was the only type of programming available. The human representation of a program was a sequence of ones and zeros (or bits). Program development was extremely difficult, tedious, and error-prone. These languages were very low-level because they consisted of machine instructions used to express very detailed manipulation at the hardware level. Consequently, they were hardware dependent.

2.2 Assembly Languages

The first group of programming languages developed includes the symbolic machine languages (also called assembly languages). These languages were designed to ease and improve the construction of programs. Assembly language is still used today for detailed control of hardware devices; it is also used when extremely efficient execution is required. In these languages, various mnemonic symbols represent operations and addresses in memory. These languages are also low-level and hardware dependent; there is a different assembly language for every computer type.

2.3 High-Level Programming Languages

The purpose of a programming language is to allow a human to write instructions to the computer in the form of a program. A programming language must be expressive enough to help the human in the writing of programs for a large family of problems.

Programming languages are described as high-level because they are hardware independent and closer to the problem (or family of problems) to be solved. They allow more readable programs that are easier to write and maintain. Examples of conventional high-level programming languages are Pascal, C, Cobol, Fortran, Algol, Ada, Smalltalk, C++, Eiffel, and Java. These last four languages are object-oriented programming languages, and they are considered slightly higher level than the other high-level languages.

The first object-oriented language, Simula, was developed in the mid-1960s. It was used mainly to write simulation models. The language is an extension of Algol. In a similar manner, C++ was developed as an extension to C in the early 1980s.

Java was developed by Sun Microsystems in the mid-1990s, as an object-oriented programming language that was an improvement of C++. Today Java has far more capabilities than any other object-oriented programming language to date.

2.4 Compilation

The solution to a problem is implemented in an appropriate programming language. This becomes the source program written in a high-level programming language, such as C++, Eiffel, and Java.

Once a source program is written, it is translated to an equivalent program in machine language, which is the only programming language that the computer can understand. The computer can only execute instructions that are in machine language.

The translation of the source program to machine language is called *compilation*. The step that follows is called *linking*, and it generates an executable program in machine language. For some other languages, like Java, the user carries out two steps: compilation and interpretation. This last step involves direct execution of the compiled program.

Figure 2.1 shows what is involved in compilation of a source program in Java. The Java compiler checks for syntax errors in the source program and then translates it into a program in *byte-code*, which is the program in an intermediate form. Because the Java byte-code is not dependent on any particular platform or computer system, it is very portable from one machine to another.

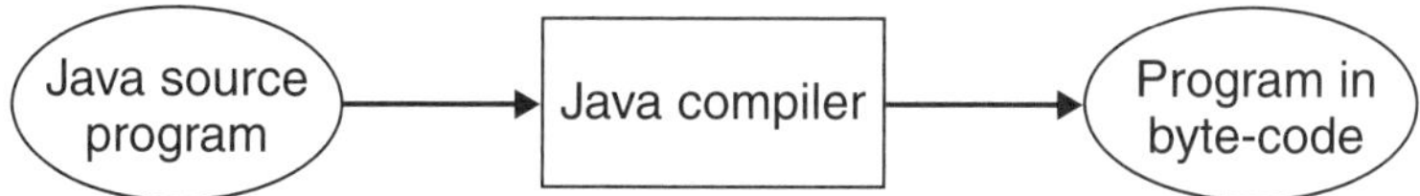

Figure 2.1 *Compiling a Java source program.*

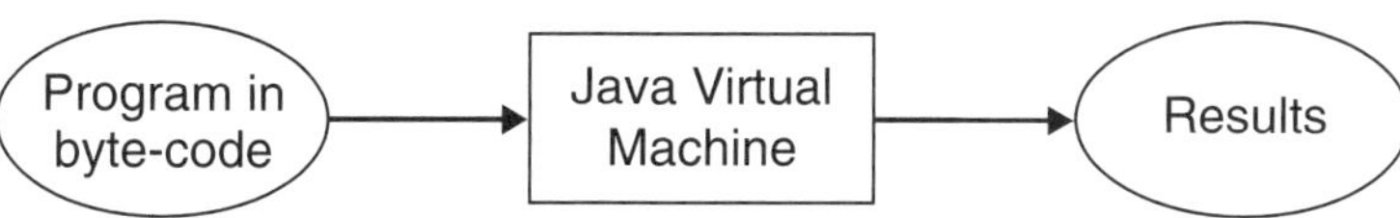

Figure 2.2 *Executing a Java program.*

Figure 2.2 shows how to execute a program in byte-code. The Java Virtual Machine (JVM), which is another software tool from Sun Microsystems, carries out the interpretation of the program in byte-code.

2.5 Program Execution

Before a program starts to execute, it must be loaded into the memory of the computer. The program executing in the computer usually reads input data from the input device, and after carrying out some computations, it writes results to the output device(s).

When executing in a computer, a program reads data from the input device (the keyboard), then carries out some transformation on the data and writes the results on the output device (the video screen). The transformation also produces intermediate results.

In a personal computer system, the input data typically originates in the user keyboard. Similarly, the output data list is directed to the computer screen. A program will read data from the input list, carry out some transformation on this data, and write output data (results) to the output list.

The instructions in a program define a set of transformations on the input data. These transformations, together with the data description, represent the program, which implements the solution.

Objects and Classes

A real-world problem can be modeled as a complex collection of entities that interact with one another and with their surroundings. When solving such a problem, a simplified representation of the problem is used to study the problem and construct a solution. This representation is called a *model* of the problem. It is composed of abstract objects and includes descriptions of their interactions, each object representing a real-world entity.

One of the main goals when developing object-oriented programs is to construct abstract representations of some aspect of the real world—a simplified description with only the relevant or essential properties of part of a real system. A model is such an abstract description of some part of the problem domain. The process of designing a model is called *modeling*. This section introduces objects and classes in modeling.

Objects—the central focus of the object-oriented approach to problem solving—are models of the real world identified in the real-world environment of the problem. Objects with similar characteristics are grouped into collections known as *classes*.

3.1 Objects

The concept of *abstraction* is applied when describing the objects of a problem. This involves the elimination of unessential characteristics. As mentioned previously, *modeling* is the task of designing and building a model. The result of modeling includes only the relevant objects and essential characteristics of these objects. There are three important issues in object-oriented modeling:

1. Identifying the objects to be included in the model
2. Describing these objects
3. Grouping objects with similar characteristics into collections of objects

3.2 Describing Objects

Objects are a dynamic concept because they exhibit independent behavior and interact with one another. They communicate by sending messages to each other; this way all objects collaborate for a common goal. Every object has three characteristics:

1. *State*, represented by the set of *properties* (or attributes) and their associated values
2. *Behavior*, represented by the operations, also known as *methods*, of the object
3. *Identity*, which is a property that can help identify an object

A collection of similar objects is called a class. Consider a simple example of an object of class `Ball`. The attributes of this object are *color*, *size*, and *status*, which is also called its `move_status`. Figure 3.1 shows a diagram for two `Ball` objects and illustrates their structure. The diagram is basically a rectangle divided into three sections. The top section indicates the class of the object, the middle section includes the list of the attributes and their current values, and the bottom section describes the behavior of the object, which is defined by a list of operations of the object.

The state of an object is defined by the value of the attributes. The value of attribute *color* is a text string, which is enclosed in quotes. The value of attribute *size* is a numeric value. The value of attribute `move_status` is a single text character, which is enclosed in apostrophes. The two objects of class `Ball` are in different states because their attributes have different values.

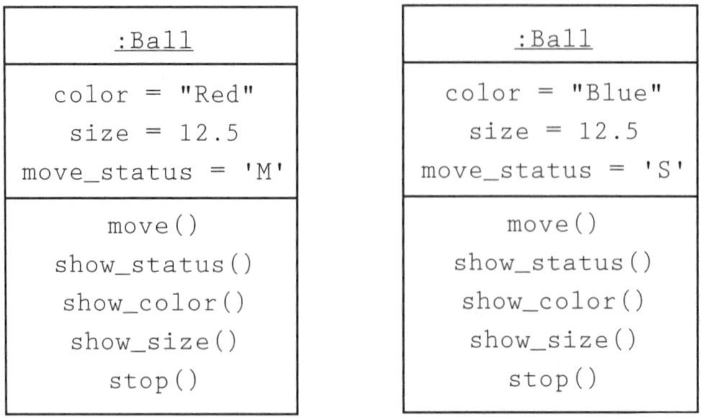

:Ball
color = "Red" size = 12.5 move_status = 'M'
move() show_status() show_color() show_size() stop()

:Ball
color = "Blue" size = 12.5 move_status = 'S'
move() show_status() show_color() show_size() stop()

Figure 3.1 *Two objects of class* `Ball`.

3.3 Object Behavior

An object exhibits behavior when one of its methods is called, or invoked. An object will normally interact with another object. This behavior is carried out by one object calling a method of another object, or one object sending a *message* to another object.

The purpose of sending a message to an object is to request that some method of the object be performed; in other words, the request is a call to one of the methods of the object. This is also known as *method invocation*. Objects carry out methods in response to messages.

These methods are object-specific; a message is always sent to a specific object. A method invocation (a message) contains three parts:

1. The name of the object
2. The name of the method or operation
3. The input data required by the method

3.4 Classes

In the real-world problem, *collections* of real-world entities or objects with similar characteristics are identified. The abstract descriptions of the collections of objects are called classes.

Figure 3.2 illustrates the identification of several collections of real-world entities, the modeling of the classes, and the software implementation of these classes. Each class is an abstract representation, a model, of a collection of similar real-world entities. Classes of such objects are used to distinguish one type of object from another. The model of a class is represented graphically as a class diagram.

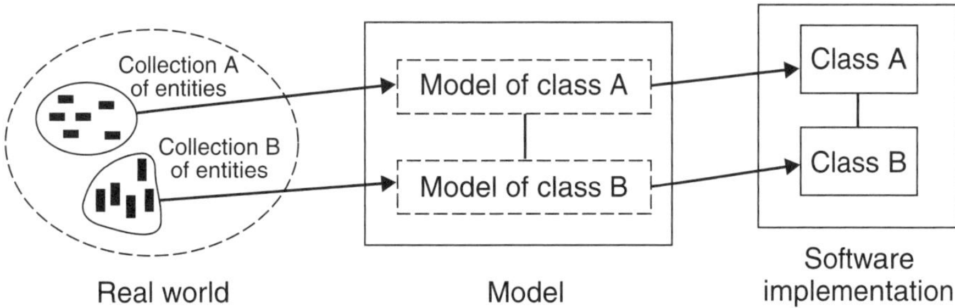

Figure 3.2 *Collections and classes.*

Figure 3.3 *Class* `Person`.

An object belongs to a collection or class, and any object of the class is an instance of the class. A class defines the attributes and behavior for all the objects of the class. Every class defines the following:

1. Attributes (data declarations)
2. One or more operations (also known as functions and methods)

A complete object-oriented model of an application consists of a description of all the classes and their relationships, the objects and their interaction, and a complete documentation of these. Figure 3.3 shows the diagram for class `Person`.

3.5 Encapsulation

An object is described as the integration of attributes and behavior in a single unit. There is an imaginary wall surrounding the object to protect it from another object. This is considered an encapsulation protection mechanism. To protect the features of an object, an access mode is specified for every feature.

Access to some of the attributes and operations is allowed if they are *public*. Some attributes and operations are not allowed to be accessed if the access mode is specified *private*. If an operation of an object is public, it is accessible from other objects.

3.6 Information Hiding

A class definition shows only the services that the object provides and hides all implementation details. For this, an object presents two views:

1. The external view, which consists of the list of services (or operations) that other objects can invoke. This list can be used as a service contract between the provider object and the client objects.
2. The internal view, which presents the implementation details of the data and the operations of the object. This information is hidden from other objects.

Why Alice?

Conventional high-level programming languages like C++ and Java can require considerable effort to learn and master. Alice is a newer programming language that is based on modern computer technology and that allows the student to interact with a three-dimensional graphical environment. This is emphasized in Figure 5.1, which shows the Alice logo.

Alice is much more than a programming language; it is an environment that allows students to explore design ideas. One of the important goals of Alice is to make it easier for students to learn object-oriented programming principles and to help them transition later to other programming languages such as C++ and Java.

Overview of Alice

Objects in Alice are three-dimensional and are visible on a graphical environment that simulates a real world. This abstract world is called a *virtual world*. The programming philosophy of Alice consists of the construction of virtual worlds, starting with a scene and then creating objects and adding them to the scene that will display their behavior via graphical animations.

5.1 First Look at Alice

The initial screen that appears when the Alice software is started by doubleclicking on its executable file name `Alice.exe` (or its shortcut on the Windows Desktop) is shown in Figure 5.1.

Figure 5.1 *Initial screen of the Alice system.*

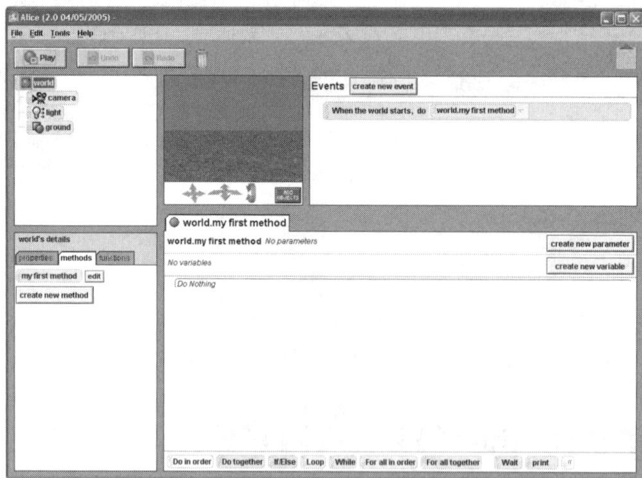

Figure 5.2 *Main window for Alice.*

It will only show for a few seconds. The main window of Alice, also called the Alice interface, is shown in Figure 5.2. The next window is the welcome screen (or dialog box) of the Alice System (Figure 5.3). It will normally appear in front of the Alice interface.

The following menus are shown on the welcome screen: `Tutorial`, `Recent Worlds`, `Templates`, `Examples`, and `Open a World`. For a person learning about Alice, the most relevant menus are the `Tutorial` and the `Examples`.

Figure 5.3 *Welcome screen of the Alice system.*

Figure 5.4 `Tutorial` *dialog box for Alice.*

If you click on the `Tutorial` tab, a new dialog box appears, as shown in Figure 5.4. This box shows the Alice tutorial with four components: `Tutorial1`, `Tutorial2`, `Tutorial3`, and `Tutorial4`. The user can start any of these subtutorials or start the entire tutorial by clicking on the `Start the Tutorial` button at the center top of the dialog box.

The `Examples` dialog box appears when the tab is selected from the Alice welcome screen. Figure 5.5 shows seven buttons, each one corresponding to a predefined virtual world: `almostAllAboutAlice`, `amusementPark`, `flightSimulator`, `lakeSkater`, `lakeSkaterDemoStart`, `LightDemo`, and `SnowLove`. This last button can be made visible by moving down the scroll bar.

Figure 5.5 `Examples` *dialog box for Alice.*

Predefined Virtual Worlds

This chapter presents an example of a predefined virtual world. Start again with the `Examples` dialog box that appears when the tab is selected from the Alice welcome screen, as shown in Figure 5.5. Select the `LightDemo` tab and click the `Open` button. The selected virtual world will start loading, and when it is ready, it will display the screen shown in Figure 6.1.

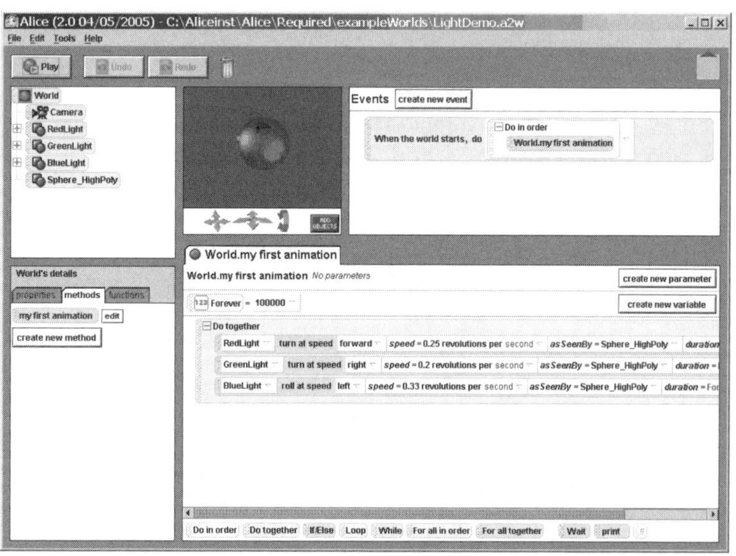

Figure 6.1 *The* `LightDemo` *example of a predefined Alice world.*

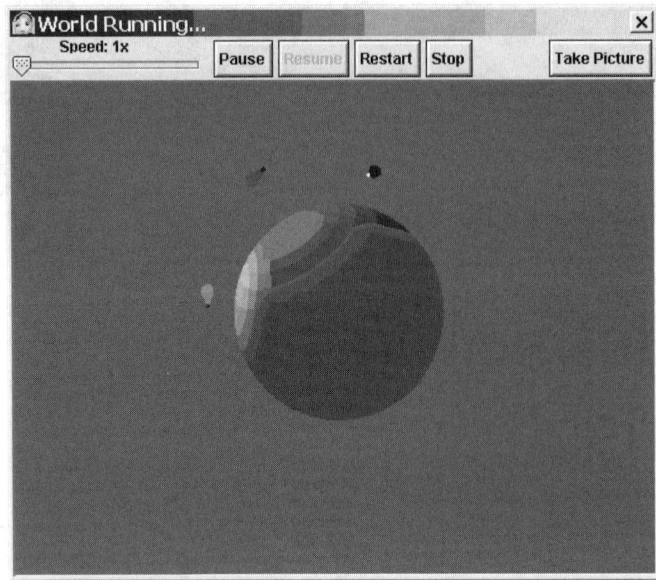

Figure 6.2 *Animation of the* `LightDemo` *Alice world.*

The `LightDemo` virtual world is a good example of an Alice world that has animation but does not include interaction with the user. To start the animation of this virtual world, click on the `Play` button on the upper-left area of the `LightDemo` window. The animation is displayed on the new window shown in Figure 6.2.

Animations in virtual worlds represent the behavior of the objects in the virtual world. This behavior is generally seen as some type of movement of the objects in a three-dimensional axis.

The animation window has a speed slider control at the top and five buttons: (1) `Pause`, (2) `Resume`, (3) `Restart`, (4) `Stop`, and (5) `Take Picture`. The speed of the animation can be changed with the slider control.

Developing a Virtual World

In Alice, a virtual world is a large object that will normally contain other (smaller) objects created and added by the user. The world object has some default properties and behavior. Developing an Alice world consists of the following steps:

1. Create an empty virtual world and define its initial properties by adding a template, which consists of a virtual environment.
2. Select one of the object classes that are available on the Alice object galleries.
3. Create a new object instantiated from the object class selected and add the object to the Alice virtual world.
4. Include the behavior of the object by defining one or more methods of the object.
5. Define the event that will start the object behavior.
6. Repeat from step 2 to include additional objects in the virtual world.
7. Start the animation of the virtual world by clicking on the `Play` button.

7.1 Creating the Initial Scene for a New World

To start developing an initial world, start the Alice system and click on the `File` menu, then select `New World`. To prepare the environment for a new world, click on the `Templates` tab. Figure 7.1 shows the dialog box with the templates available for creating a new virtual world. Select `dirt` and click the `Open` button in the bottom-right corner of the dialog box.

Figure 7.2 shows the initial scene of the new virtual world created with the `dirt` template. Only two parts of the complete Alice interface are shown in the figure. On the left side, the object tree is shown, which indicates how the objects are organized in the virtual world. On the right side, the world view is shown with the selected template (`dirt`). At the bottom-right corner of the world view, a green button is shown with the label `Add Objects`.

7.2 Selecting an Object Class from the Object Galleries

To select an object class from an object gallery, open an object gallery. Click on the `Add Objects` button, which is a green button located at the bottom-right corner of the world view (as shown in Figure 7.2).

Figure 7.3 shows the three galleries normally available on the Alice system: `Local Gallery`, `CD Gallery`, and `Web Gallery`.

The default is the `Local Gallery`, part of which is shown in Figure 7.4. From this point on, this will appear in the bottom part of the Alice interface.

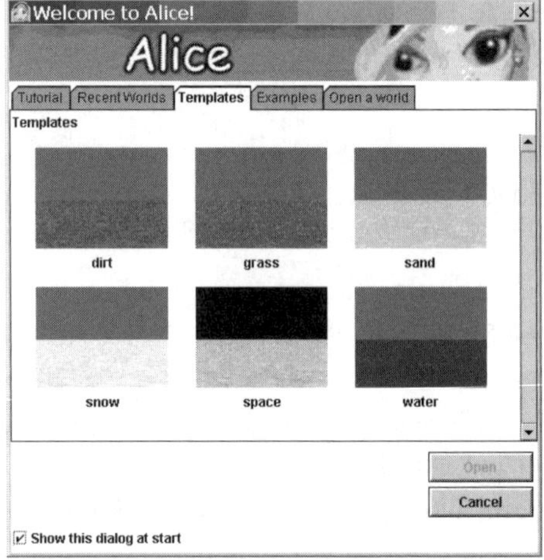

Figure 7.1 *Dialog box with the Alice templates.*

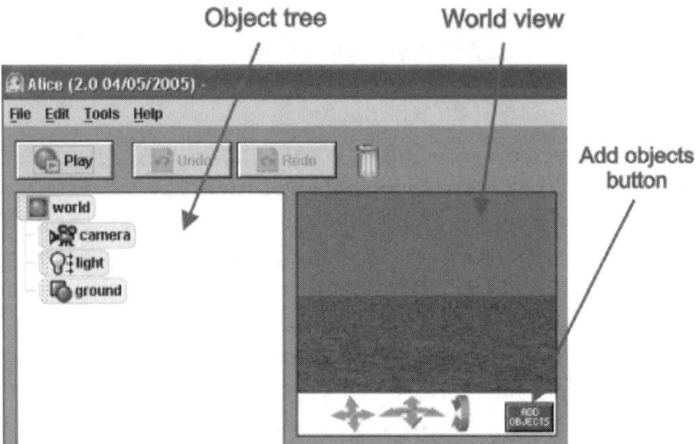

Figure 7.2 *Initial scene of an Alice world with the* `dirt` *template.*

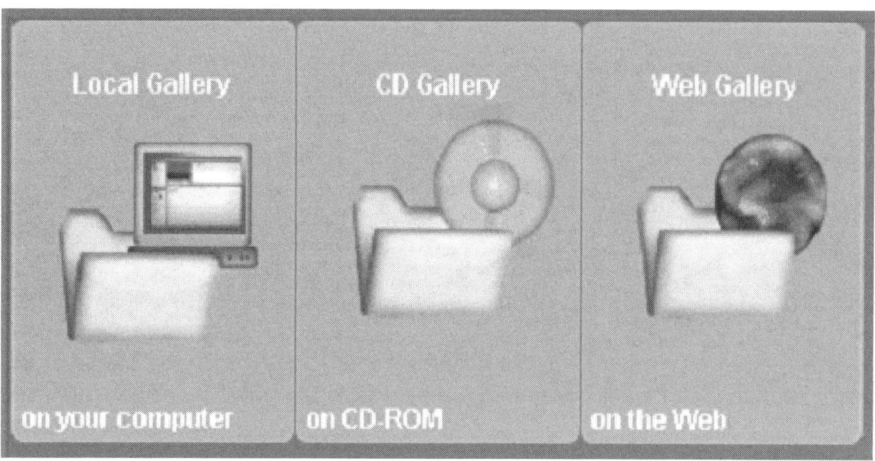

Figure 7.3 *The three galleries available on Alice.*

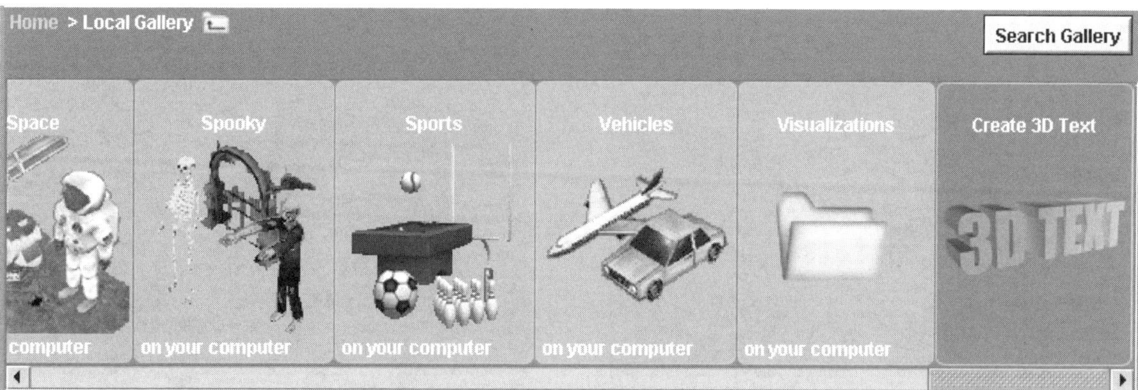

Figure 7.4 *Partial view of the local object gallery.*

The rest of the gallery becomes visible by scrolling left or right with the scroll bar below the gallery folders.

For example, search the local gallery and select `Vehicles` by clicking on its icon. This opens the `Vehicles` folder, which contains the various vehicles classes (see Figure 7.5).

When any class is selected from the `Vehicles` folder, Alice will show a small window or box with relevant data about the class. Figure 7.6 shows the information window for class `Humvee` and class `Corvette` from the `Vehicles` folder.

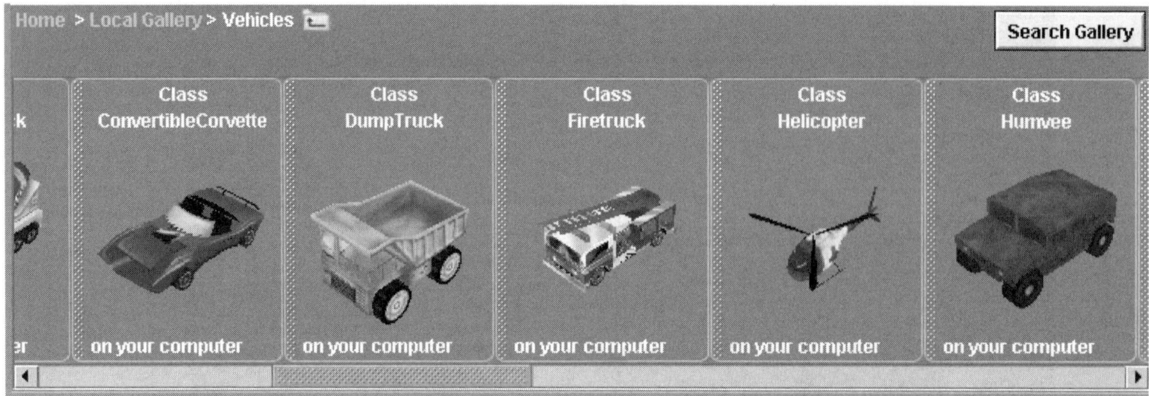

Figure 7.5 *Partial view of the* `Vehicles` *class in the local object gallery.*

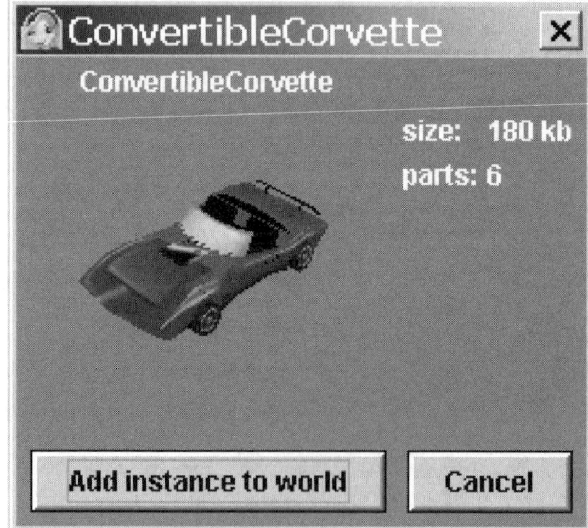

Figure 7.6 *Information window for class* `Humvee` *and class* `Corvette`.

7.3 Creating and Adding Objects

To create and add new objects to a virtual world, the selected object class has to be instantiated. This is carried out by clicking the `Add instance to world` button on the information window of class `Humvee`. The Alice system will place a `Humvee` object into the current virtual world. Figure 7.7 shows the virtual world with the Humvee on the dirt on the left side.

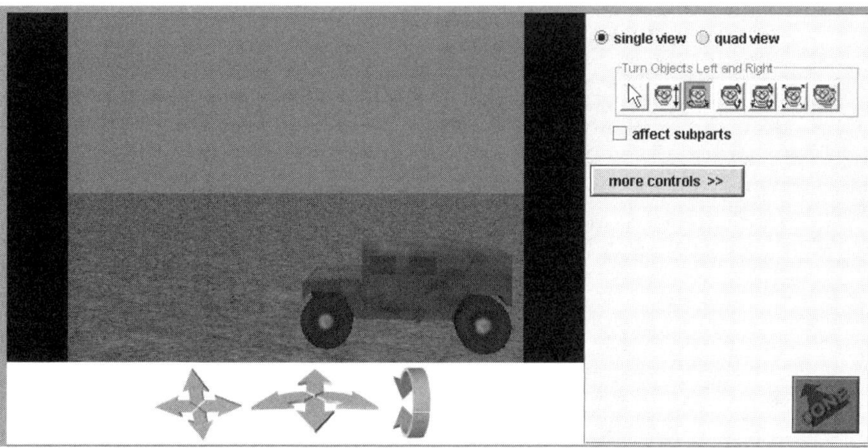

Figure 7.7 *An object of class* `Humvee` *in a virtual world.*

In order to reposition the object at the appropriate place in the world, seven layout tools, shown on the right side of Figure 7.7, can be used to manipulate the position of the objects: (1) `Pointer` tool, (2) `Vertical` tool, (3) `Turn` tool, (4) `Rotate` tool, (5) `Tumble` tool, (6) `Resize` tool, and (7) `Duplicate` tool. Note that the `humvee` object has been moved to the right side of the virtual world, facing to the left. The entire Alice interface with the `humvee` object is shown in Figure 7.8.

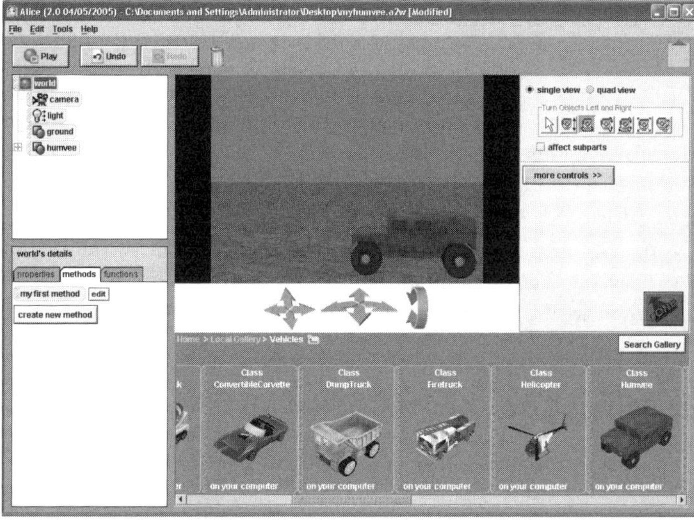

Figure 7.8 *Alice interface with an object of class* `Humvee`.

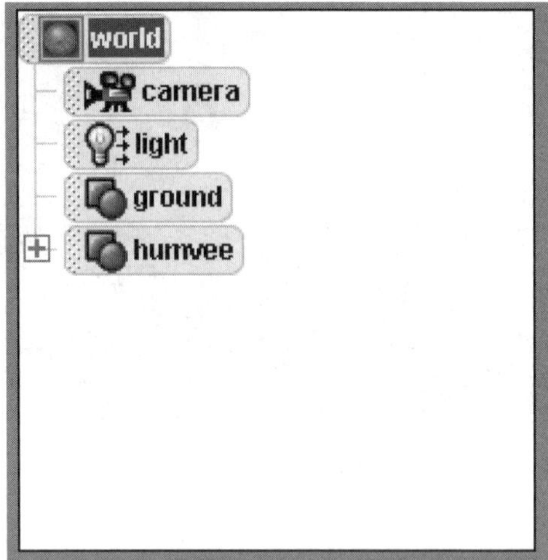

Figure 7.9 *World object tree with an object of class* `Humvee`.

Since no more objects are going to be added to the current world in this example, click on the green button with the red label `Done`, which is on the right side of Figure 7.8. Note that the `humvee` object has been added to the world's object tree, as shown in the upper-left pane in Figure 7.8 and illustrated in more detail in Figure 7.9.

7.4 Including Object Behavior

Animation in Alice is accomplished by specifying some *actions* to be performed by the objects that were added from the galleries. The behavior of objects is defined by the actions specified in each class of objects. The object behavior includes a definition of what possible actions the objects of the class are capable of performing. Every class includes two types of features: *attributes* (also called *properties*) and *methods*. The actions are specified as the methods of the objects of the class. The default method of the current world (`world.myfirstmethod`) is shown in the details pane of the world located in the lower-left pane in Figure 7.8.

Specifying the Object Behavior

The actual object behavior depends on the algorithm design. Recall that an algorithm is a step-by-step description of the operations to perform in order to complete a task or solve a problem. Assume that the following sequence of actions is to be performed by the `humvee` object:

```
Perform the following steps in sequence
    Move forward 1.5 meters
    Turn right 0.2 revolutions
    Move forward 2.5 meters
    Move backward 1 meter
    Turn left 0.2 revolutions
    Move forward 1.5 meters
```

The actions specified for the `humvee` object now need to be implemented in Alice in the given order. Each of these actions can be carried out by one or more of the methods of the `humvee` object. To view the methods provided by Alice for an object of class `Humvee`, select the object `humvee` on the object tree pane in the upper-left pane of Figure 7.8. The methods of this object are shown in the lower-left pane of the figure. A partial view of the methods of object `humvee` is shown in the `humvee's details` in Figure 7.10. Scrolling down the bar will show the rest of the methods.

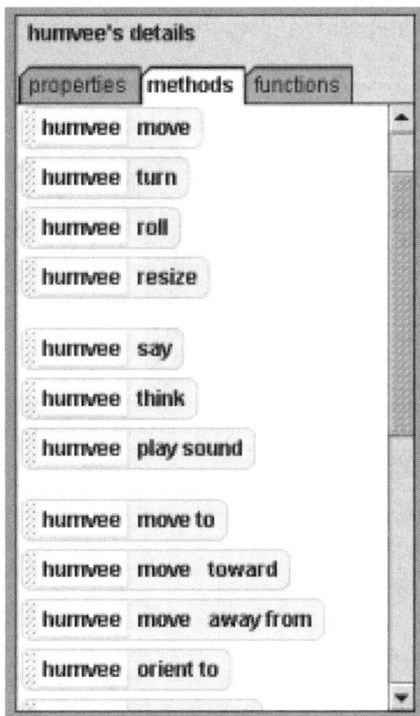

Figure 7.10 *Methods of an object of class* `Humvee`.

Constructing an Alice Program

The code part of a program has several fundamental components:

1. Instructions
2. Control structures
3. Functions
4. Expressions

Not all these components are required for simple programs. To construct a simple program in Alice with the `humvee` object, each action specified for the object is translated into Alice instructions using one or more of the object's methods. This consists of dragging the tile of every method required of the object shown in Figure 7.10 and placing it in the right sequence in the code `Editor` shown in the lower right of Figure 7.11. These Alice instructions will basically be used to code the main method of the current Alice world.

The `control statements` are selected from the bottom line of the `Editor` area. The tile of a selected control statement is dragged into the `Editor` area where the Alice program is being constructed. The `Editor` is shown with more detail in Figure 7.12.

For the specified sequence of instructions needed to implement basic behavior of the `humvee` object, the only control sequence required is `Do in order`. This statement allows the programmer to specify the execution of a

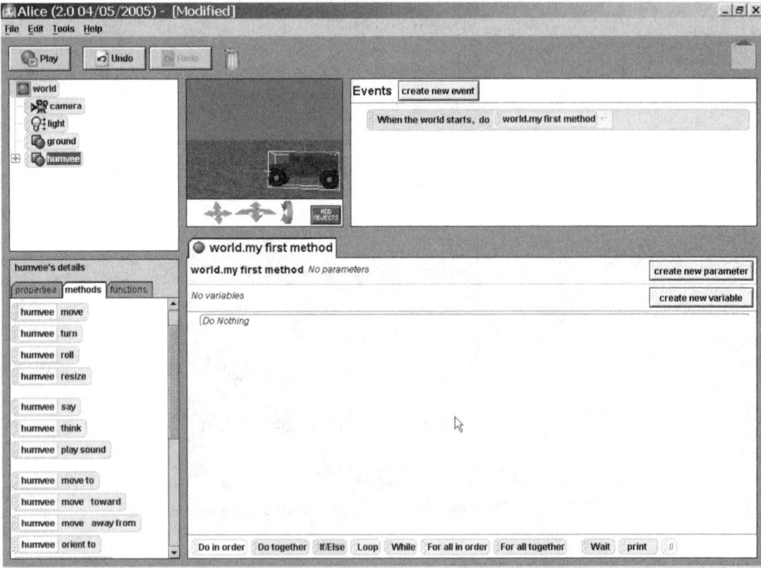

Figure 7.11 *Alice world with* `Humvee` *object.*

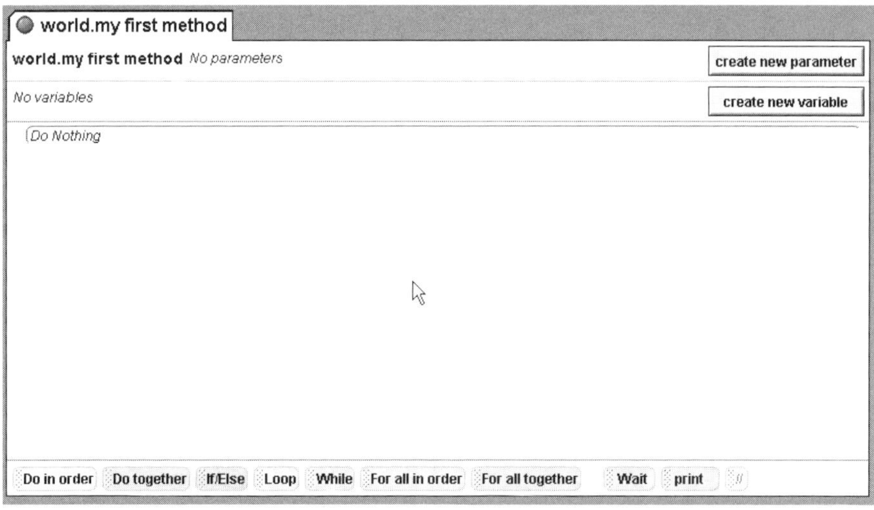

Figure 7.12 `Editor` *area of an Alice world.*

block of methods as a sequence, one method after the other and from top to bottom. The tile of the `Do in order` statement is located in the bottom-left side of the `Editor` area, as shown in Figure 7.12.

To completely implement the basic behavior of object `humvee`, the tile of every method from the `humvee's details` pane (Figure 7.10) is dragged into the `Editor` area.

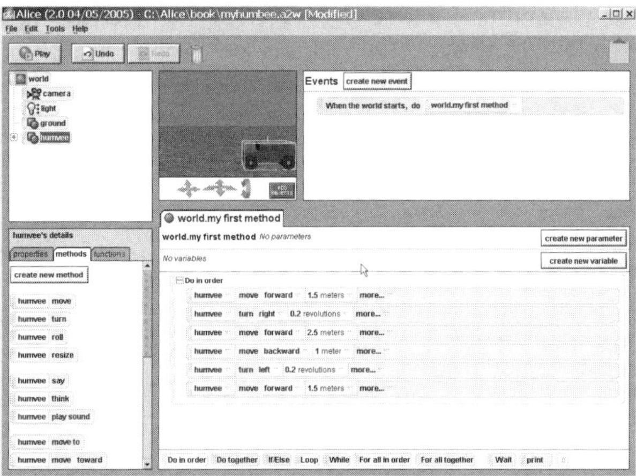

Figure 7.13 *An Alice world with* `Humvee` *object and the complete* `Editor` *area.*

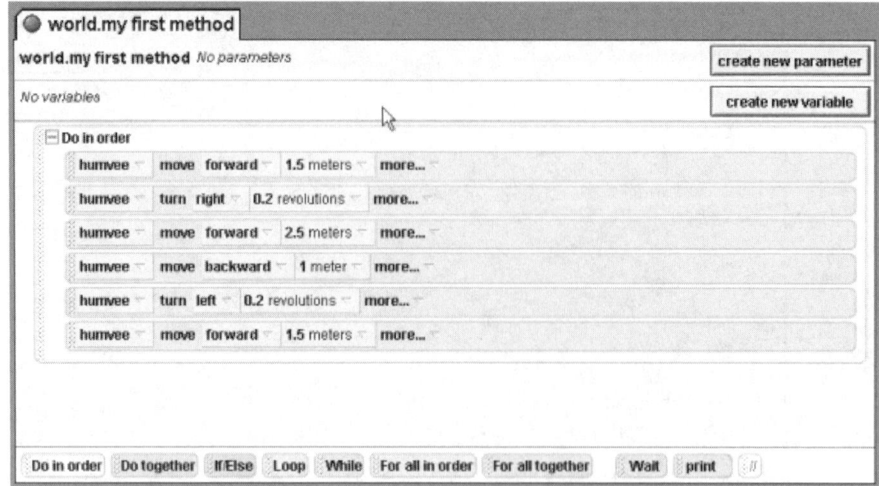

Figure 7.14 `Editor` *area with methods.*

Figure 7.13 shows the Alice world with the `humvee` object and the methods needed. Figure 7.14 shows the details of the `Editor` area.

7.5 Running the Animation

The Alice program for the example discussed has been implemented as a set of instructions that provide behavior of the object of class `Humvee`. This behavior was first specified as a set of actions for object `humvee`. These actions were then implemented using the methods of class `Humvee`.

To view the animation, run the Alice world constructed by clicking on the `Play` button located on the upper-left side of the Alice world shown in Figure 7.13. When the animation starts running, the object `humvee` moves as directed by the instruction specified.

Simultaneous Actions

In the previous example, the actions of object humvee were to be executed one after another—in other words, in sequential order. Playing the animation again clearly shows that the move action of the object is executed before the turn right action.

Some of the actions of object humvee can be performed simultaneously. For example, the object can be made to turn left and at the same time to move forward. Consider a modified behavior specified for object humvee. The new behavior of the object will now include (1) a few actions of object humvee that are to occur in sequence and (2) some actions that are to occur simultaneously. These simultaneous actions are move forward and turn left and are to occur after the sequential actions. The following is an informal description of the modified actions of object humvee.

```
Perform the following steps in sequence
    Move forward 1.5 meters
    Turn right 0.2 revolutions
    Move forward 2.5 meters
    Move backward 2 meters
    Perform the following steps simultaneously
        Turn left 0.2 revolutions
        Move forward 2 meters
```

As indicated previously, to construct a simple program in Alice with the humvee object, each action specified for the object is translated into Alice instructions using one or more of the object's methods. This consists of dragging the tile of every method required of the object shown in Figure 7.10 and placing it in the right sequence in the code Editor of the Alice world shown in Figure 8.1.

The control statements are selected from the bottom line of the Editor area. The tile of a selected control statement is dragged into the Editor area where the Alice program is being constructed.

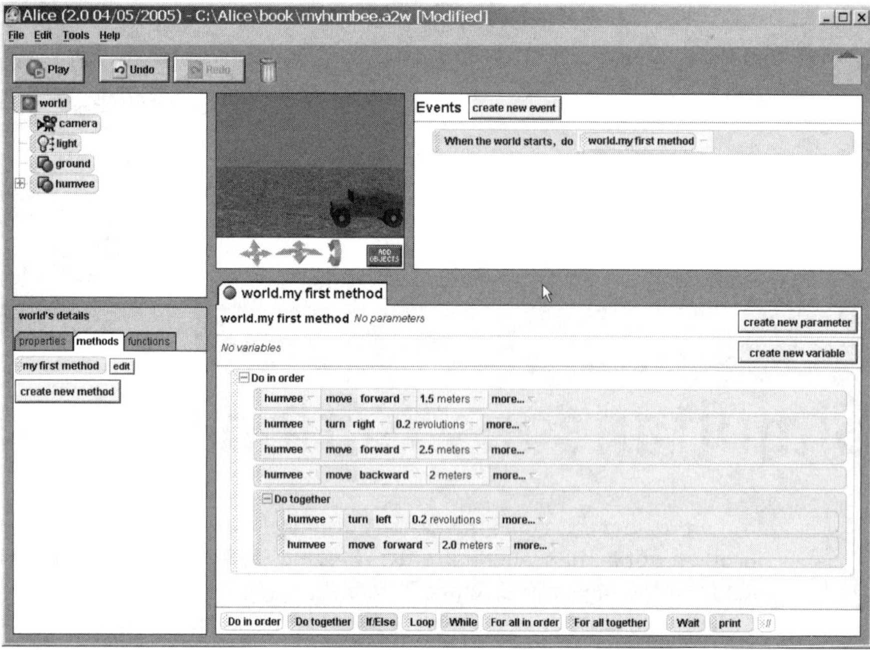

Figure 8.1 *New Alice world with modified behavior of object* `humvee`.

Alice allows the specification of actions that occur simultaneously. To implement this type of behavior in Alice, the `Do together` control statement is used. Figure 8.2 shows the `Editor` area with actions implemented for object `humvee`.

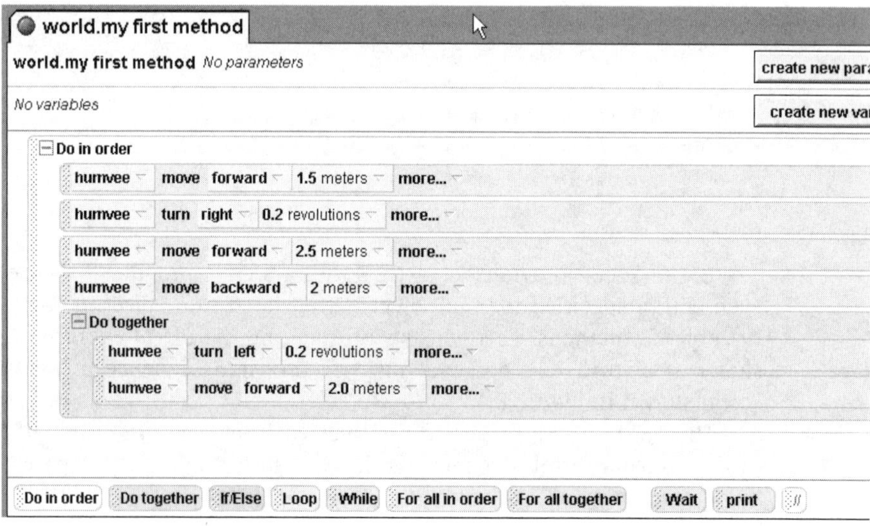

Figure 8.2 `Editor` *area with methods for simultaneous actions.*

To view the animation, run the Alice world constructed by clicking on the `Play` button located on the upper-left side of the Alice world shown in Figure 8.1. When the animation starts running, object `humvee` moves as directed by the instruction specified.

Notations for Algorithm Description

Recall that an algorithm is a detailed step-by-step description of how to carry out a task or how to solve a problem. There are several types of notations that are widely used to describe an algorithm:

1. Informal English
2. Flowcharts
3. Pseudocode

9.1 Informal English

This is the most natural and easy notation to describe an algorithm. The main disadvantages of this notation are that the resulting description is very ambiguous and it does not clearly represent the detailed steps of the algorithm logic.

9.2 Flowcharts

A flowchart is a visual tool for describing the order of how steps or instructions are to be performed. It consists of a set of symbols connected by arrows showing the order in which the instructions are to be performed, as well as the flow of data.

Figure 9.1 shows some of the basic symbols used in flowcharts, including the arrows that connect these symbols. The most general symbol is the *process symbol,* a rectangular box that represents any computation or sequence of actions to be executed on some data. There is one arrow pointing in and one arrow pointing out of the symbol.

Another symbol shown in Figure 9.1 has the shape of a vertical rhombus (or diamond), and it represents a selection of alternate paths in the instruction flow. This symbol is also

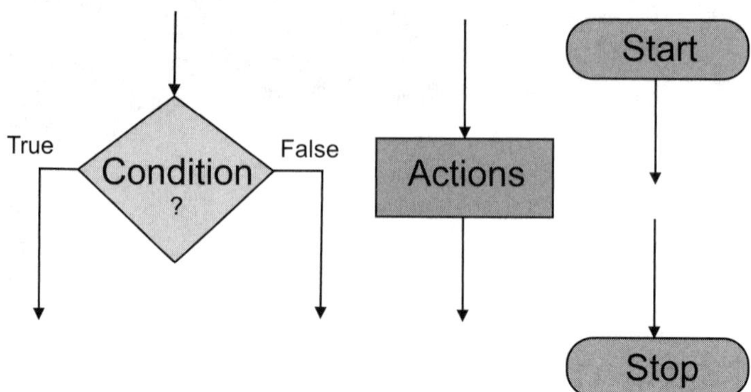

Figure 9.1 *Basic symbols used in flowcharts.*

known as a *decision block* or a *conditional block* because the sequence of instructions can take one of two directions in the flowchart, depending on the *evaluation* of the condition. A flowchart normally begins with a *start symbol,* and ends with a *stop symbol.* The start symbol has an arrow pointing out of it, and the stop symbol has one arrow pointing into it.

9.3 Pseudocode

Pseudocode is structured notation that can be very informal; it uses English description of the set of transformations that define a problem solution. It is a natural language description of an algorithm.

Pseudocode is much easier to understand and use than an actual programming language. The main advantage of pseudocode over flowcharts is that it can be used to describe relatively large and complex algorithms.

If a few design rules are followed, another advantage is that it is easy to convert the pseudocode to the code of a programming language. The notation used in a programming language is much more formal and allows the programmer to clearly and precisely describe the algorithm in detail.

Several levels of algorithm descriptions are normally necessary, from a very general level for describing a preliminary design to a much more detailed description for describing a final design.

Variables

A variable is a memory location that has a name and can store some value. The value of a variable changes during the execution of the program. For every computation, there is at least one associated variable that is to be used by the computations (computer operations).

Variables appear in the classes as attribute declarations. Similar data definitions appear within the functions and methods; these are known as *local* variables.

Simple variables are those of simple or primitive types; these store small and simple data items such as integer values and floating-point values. Object variables (or object references) are variables that can store the reference to objects when they are created. Variable descriptions include the following:

1. The variable type
2. A unique name to identify the variable
3. An optional initial value

The name of a variable is an identifier and is given by the programmer; it must be different from any keyword in the programming language. The type of a variable defines two sets:

1. Possible values that the variable may have
2. Possible operations that can be applied to the variable

10.1 Names of Variables

The symbols used in an algorithm to identify the variables are called *identifiers,* and they are defined by the programmer. The unique name or label that is assigned to every variable is an identifier.

Let's consider an example: A problem for calculating the area of a triangle that needs five variables: *x*, *y*, *z*, *s*, and *area*. Because the values of variables usually change during the execution of a program, the following sequence of instructions first sets the value of *x*, then adds the value *x* to *y*, then increments the value of *x*:

```
set x to value 2          // set value of x
add x to y
increment x
```

The variables *x* and *y* have their values changed when operations are applied on them. Those variables that do not change their values are called *constants* and are given names that start with an uppercase letter—for example, `Max_period` and `PI`. These variables are given an initial value that will never change.

During the execution of a program, the variables used by the various computations are stored in memory. Every variable occupies a different memory location. The names of these variables represent symbolic memory locations.

10.2 Data Types

There are two broad groups of data types:

1. Simple (or primitive) data types
2. Classes, or types for objects

Simple types are classified into three categories:

1. Numeric
2. Text
3. Boolean

The numeric type is further divided into three subtypes: *integer*, *float*, and *double*. The noninteger types are also known as fractional types, which means that the numerical values have a fractional part.

Values of type *integer* are those that are countable to a finite value—for example, age, number of automobiles, and number of pages in a book. Values of type *float* have a decimal point—for example, cost of an item, height of a building, current temperature in a room, and time interval (period). These values cannot be expressed as integers. Values of type *double* provide more precision than type *float*—for example, the value of the total assets of a corporation.

Text variables are of type *string*, and they consist of a sequence of characters. The values for these two types of variables are textual values.

A third type of variables is the one in which the values of the variables can take a truth-value (true or false); these variables are of type *boolean*.

Classes are more complex types that appear as types of object variables in all object-oriented programs. Data entities declared (and created) with classes are called *objects*.

10.3 Defining and Using Variables in Alice

Defining Variables

To define variables in Alice, start in the `Editor` area of an Alice world and click the `create new variable` button, which is located on the right side of the `Editor` area, as shown in Figure 10.1.

Figure 10.2 shows the dialog box that appears after clicking the `create new variable` button. The dialog box asks the user for the name of the variable, a selection for the type of the variable (`Number`, `Boolean`, `Object`, `Other`), and an initial value for the variable. In the figure, a variable is defined with name `y`, of type `Number`, and an initial value of `1`. Clicking the `OK` button will finalize creating the variable and the declaration of the variable will appear on the top line of the code.

A second variable is created with name `x`, of type `Number`, and an initial value of `25`.

Changing the Value of a Variable

To change the value of a variable in Alice, drag the tile of the declaration of the variable down to the line where the instruction will appear. An option box

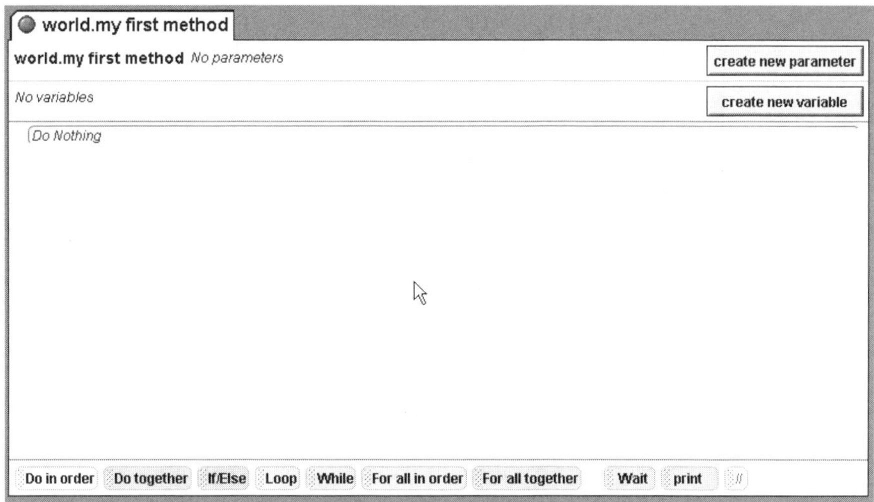

Figure 10.1 *The* `create new variable` *button in the* `Editor` *area of an Alice world.*

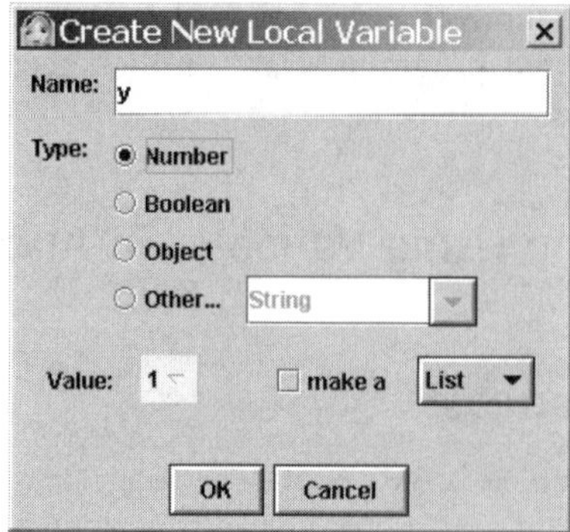

Figure 10.2 *Dialog box for defining a variable in Alice.*

appears with the three options: `set value`, `increment by 1`, and `decrement by 1`.

For example, to set the value of variable `x` to `3`, select the first option in the option box and then value `3`. Then follow the right selection box and select `Other`, then type `3` from the numeric key pad that appears. Figure 10.3 shows the options box that appears when setting the value of a variable. Note that the figure also shows the two variables that have been defined, `x` and `y`.

After setting the value `3` to variable `x` and incrementing the value of variable `y`, the following instructions will appear in the `Editor` area, as shown in Figure 10.4:

```
x set value to 3
y increment by 1
```

To set an expression to a variable, drag down the tile of the variable to the appropriate instruction line. Select `set value` and then select `expression`. For example, assume the variables `x`, `y`, and `z` have been defined. Suppose the

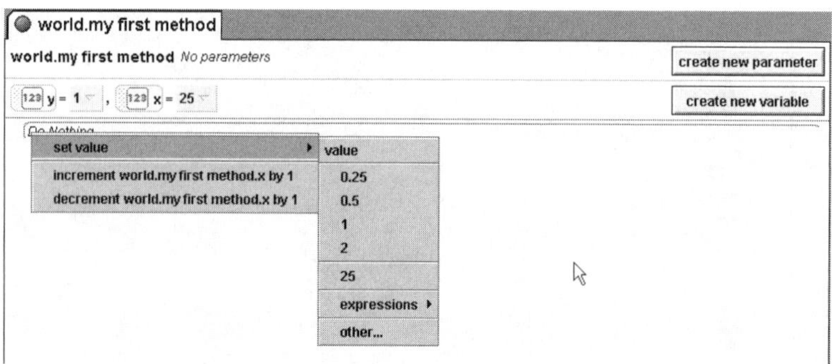

Figure 10.3 *Option box for setting the value to a variable in Alice.*

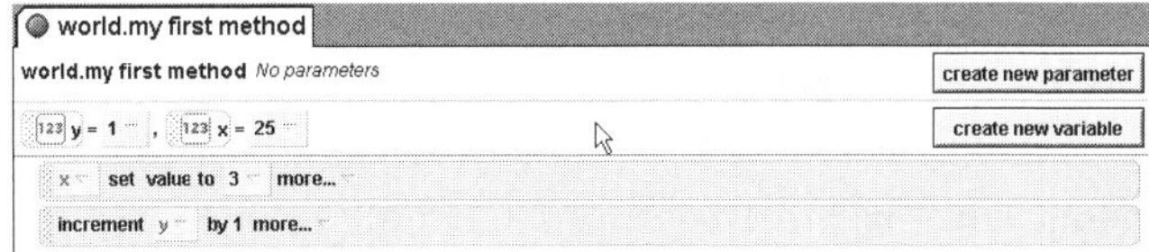

Figure 10.4 `Editor` *area after changing the value of variables* `x` *and* `y`.

expression for setting the value of variable `z` is `z = x + y`. The following steps build this expression:

1. Drag the tile of variable `z` down to the appropriate instruction line.
2. Select the `set value` option from the option box.
3. Select `expression` from the second selection box.
4. Select `x` because the expression starts with variable `x`.
5. Click on the variable `x` to continue constructing the expression, and select `math`.
6. When another option box appears, select `x+` (see Figure 10.5).
7. Select `expression` again, then `y`.

The complete resultant expression that sets the value of variable `z` will appear on the instruction line.

The final set of instructions for defining and changing the values of variables `x`, `y`, and `z` is shown in Figure 10.6.

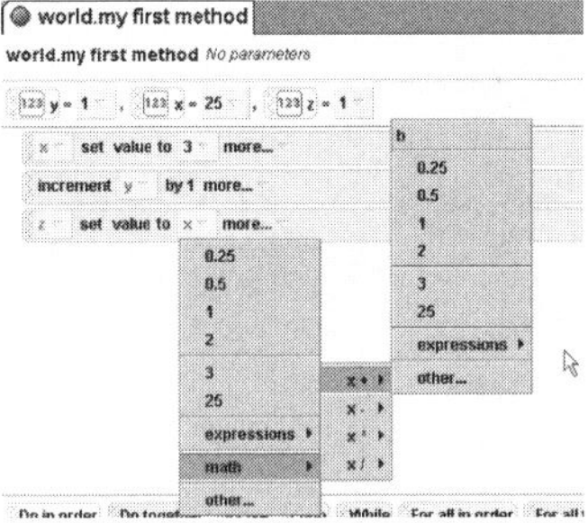

Figure 10.5 *Option box for assigning an expression to a variable in Alice.*

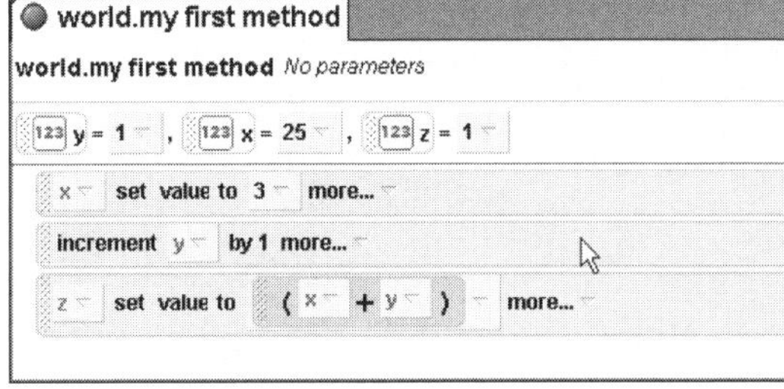

Figure 10.6 *Expressions that set the values of variables in Alice.*

10.4 Random Numbers

Random numbers are used in programming to include some unpredictability in the behavior of an object. For example, suppose the first action of the `humvee` object is to move forward a random distance of between 1 and 7 meters.

In Alice, a world function is invoked to generate a random number. The best way to accomplish this is first to create a numeric variable that will store the random value and then to use the *set* command in Alice to change the value of this variable by invoking function *random* by dragging the function's tile from the world's details pane.

Figure 10.7 shows the `world's details` (left pane) with the `random number` function. The tile of this function has been dragged into the value tile of the variable `distance` on the `Editor` area (right pane). To set the range of the random value, click on `more` on the random number tile and set the minimum value to `0.5`, then click `more` again to set the maximum value to `2.5`.

The program needs to use the variable `distance` to move the `humvee` object forward. Click on the `humvee` object in the object tree (upper-left pane of the Alice interface). On the `humvee's details` (lower-left pane), drag the `humvee move` tile to the `Editor` area. Select `forward`, then `expression`, then `distance`.

Figure 10.8 shows the `Editor` area in Alice that shows the variable `distance` set to a random value and `humvee`'s method `move` that uses this variable.

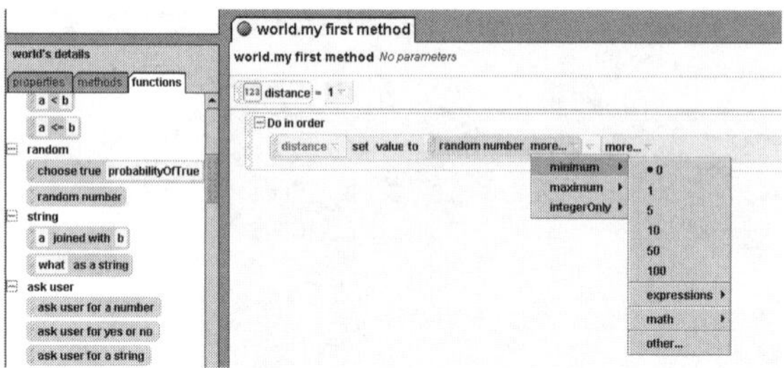

Figure 10.7 *Setting a random value of a variable in Alice.*

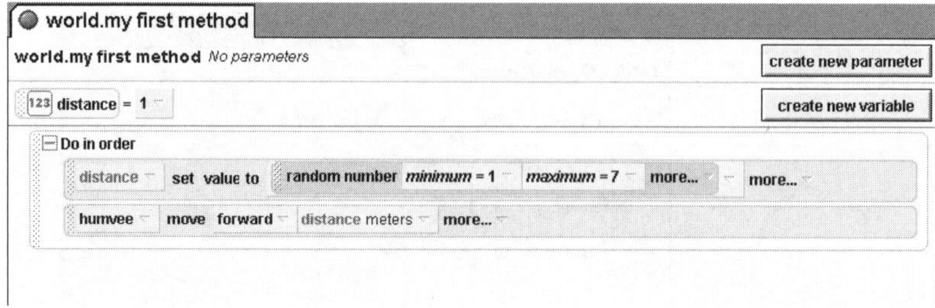

Figure 10.8 *Variable* `distance` *and* `humvee` *method* `move`.

Control Structures

Control structures are programming language statements that allow the programmer to describe how the instructions are to be executed.

In the previous sections, two control statements in Alice were used: `Do in order` and `Do together`.

An algorithm can be described using four control (logic) structures, expressed with pseudocode and/or flowcharts:

1. *Sequence,* which indicates a sequential ordering of execution of the instructions.
2. *Selection,* which indicates alternation or conditional branch; the algorithm selects one of the alternate paths depending on the evaluation of the condition.
3. *Repetition,* also called *loops,* which indicates a set (or block) of instructions that are executed zero, one, or more times.
4. *Input-output,* which are the values of indicated variables that are taken from an input device (keyword) or the values of the variables (results) that are written to an output device (screen).

11.1 Sequence

Figure 11.1 illustrates the first structure, a flowchart with a simple sequence of three actions. Each action is shown in a separate rectangular box. This is the most common and basic structure. The first example with the `humvee` discussed previously was implemented with a sequence of instructions. In Alice the control statement used is `Do in order`.

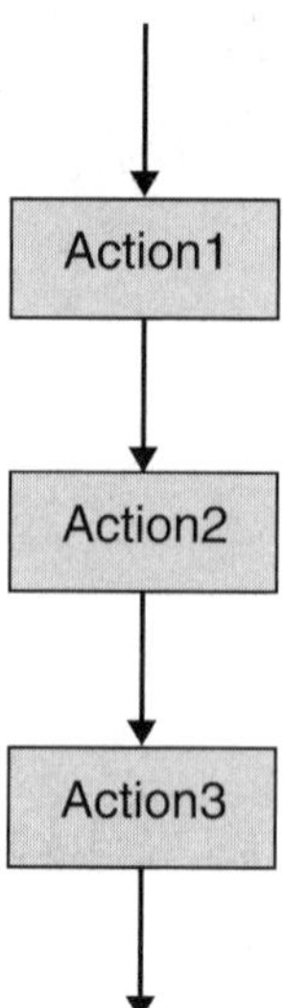

Figure 11.1 *Flowchart with a sequence of three actions.*

11.2 Selection

The selection control structure is also called alternation because alternate paths are considered based on the evaluation of a condition. The condition is examined (or evaluated) and a decision is made to select one of the paths.

Using a Flowchart

Figure 11.2 shows two possible paths for the execution flow. If the condition is true, then the left path is taken and the instruction on this path (`Action1`) will be executed. If the condition is not true, the other path is taken and the instructions on this path (`Action2`) will be executed.

Figure 11.2 illustrates a flowchart with the selection control structure. One of two alternate paths will be followed based on the evaluation of the condition. The instructions in `Action1` are executed when the condition is true. The instructions in `Action2` are executed when the condition is false.

Using Pseudocode

In the pseudocode notation, the selection structure is written with an *if statement,* also called an *if-then-else statement.* This statement includes several keywords: **if**, **then**, **else**, and **endif**. The keywords used in the pseudocode are boldfaced to clarify their usage. The **if** statement is considered a compound statement.

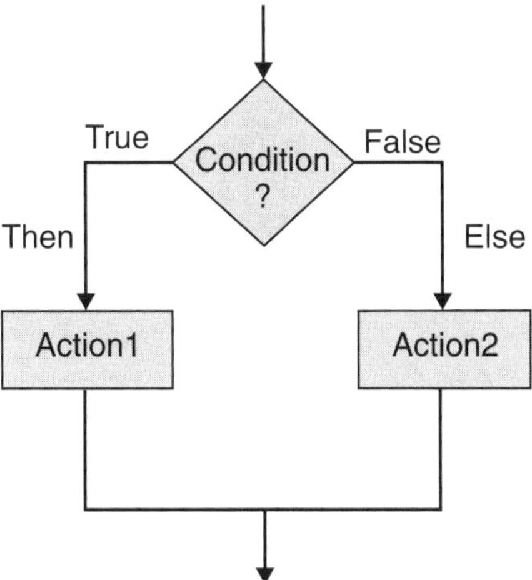

Figure 11.2 *Flowchart with selection control structure.*

All the instructions in `Action1` are said to be in the then-section of the **if** statement. In a similar manner, all the instructions in `Action2` are said to be in the else-section of the **if** statement.

The (informal) pseudocode for the **if** statement that corresponds to the general selection structure illustrated in Figure 11.1 is

```
if condition is true
   then
      perform instructions in Action1
   else
      perform instructions in Action2
endif
```

When the **if** statement executes, the condition is evaluated and only one of the two alternatives will be carried out: the one with the statements in `Action1` or the one with the statements in `Action2`.

Variations of the General Selection Structure

Figure 11.3 shows a slight variation of the selection structure. If the condition evaluates to true, the instructions in `Action1` are executed. If the condition evaluates to false, no instructions are executed, so the flow of control continues normally.

Another variation has multiple alternate paths, with each one depending on the value of a variable. This control structure is known as the *case* construct and is shown in Figure 11.4.

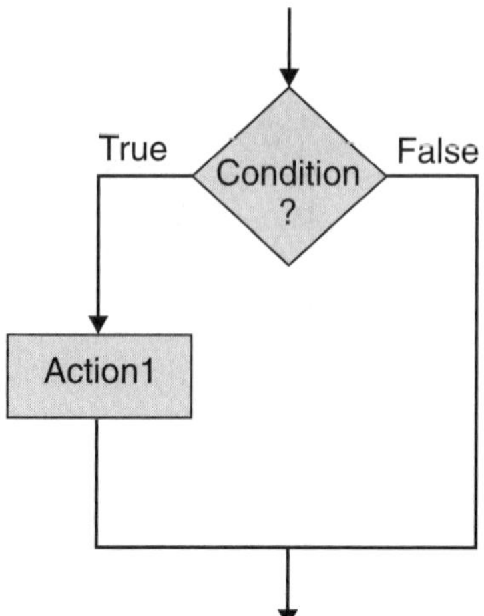

Figure 11.3 *Flowchart with a variation of the selection structure.*

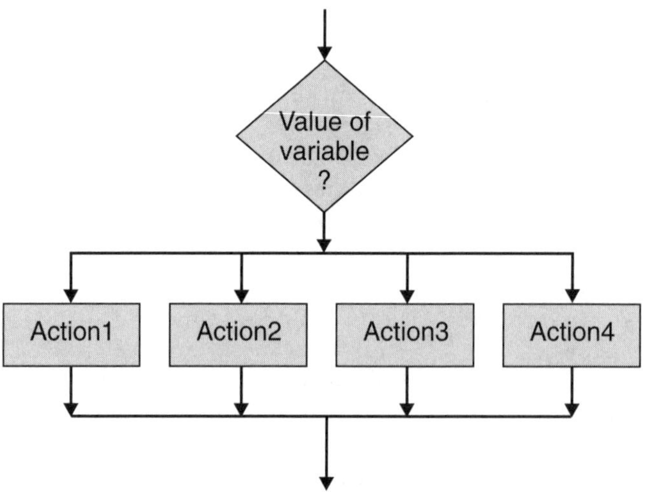

Figure 11.4 *Flowchart with selection using multiple paths.*

11.3 Conditions and Operators

Conditions are included in several control structures. A condition consists of an expression that evaluates to a truth-value, **true** or **false**. These types of expressions are also known as Boolean expressions. A simple Boolean expression compares the value of two variables.

Simple Conditional Expressions

A Boolean expression compares the two variables using a relational operator. There are six *relational operators* that are commonly used in programming languages:

1. Equal, ==
2. Not equal, !=
3. Less than, <
4. Less than or equal to, <=
5. Greater than, >
6. Greater than or equal to, >=

The following are examples of simple conditions that can be expressed with the relational operators:

```
X >= Y
p != q
wlevel <= 25.5
```

With pseudocode, additional keywords can be used instead of applying the mathematical symbols shown above for the relational operators. For example,

```
X greater than or equal to Y
p not equal to q
wlevel less than or equal to b
```

Compound Conditional Expressions

Compound expressions can be constructed with the logical operators **and**, **or**, and **not**. These operators help to join two or more simple conditions to construct conditions that are more complex. The general structure of a compound condition using the **or** operator and the two simple conditions `cond1` and `cond2` is

```
cond1 or cond2
```

The other two logical operators are used in the same manner. For example,

```
if a != b and x > 0
then
   ⟨actions_1⟩
else
   ⟨actions_2⟩
endif
```

The same compound condition above can be constructed in a more verbose manner. For example:

```
if a not equal b and x greater than 0
   ...
```

The following expression uses the **not** operator:

```
not (x <= y)
```

This expression has the following descriptive meaning: It is not true that `x` is less than or equal to `y`.

11.4 Using Selection in Alice

This section introduces the selection control structure using the **if** statement in Alice. The explanations include the application of random numbers, which were introduced in Section 10.4. This is used to implement the desired behavior of object `humvee`.

In specifying the behavior of object `humvee`, the selection control structure is needed to select the direction of the turn action of the object. The two possible actions of the object are (1) turn left or (2) turn right, depending on the distance traveled by the object.

Description of the Object Behavior in Pseudocode

The following pseudocode describes the desired behavior of object `humvee`:

```
Perform the following steps in sequence
    Set distance to a random value between 1 and 7
    Move forward for the random value in the distance variable
    if distance is less or equal to 1.5 then
       Perform the following steps simultaneously (together)
          Turn left 0.2 revolutions
          Move forward 2 meters
    else
       Perform the following steps simultaneously (together)
          Turn right 0.2 revolutions
          Move forward 2 meters
    endif
```

The If/Else Control Structure in Alice

To implement the specification of the behavior of object `humvee`, create the variable `distance` (see Section 10.4), set a random number as the value to this variable, and include the `humvee move` instruction with the distance variable.

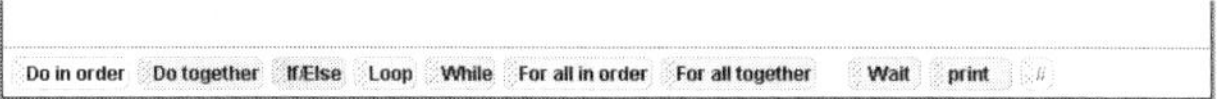

Figure 11.5 *Control statements located on the bottom of the* `Editor` *area.*

Figure 11.6 *Alice code using the* `If/Else` *statement.*

The next step is to drag the **If/Else** tile from the bottom of the `Editor` area (see Figure 11.5) and drop it below the second line of code (`humvee move` statement). When an option box appears, select `true`. Drag the tile of variable `distance` from the top line and drop it into the tile with `true` for the **If** statement. An option box appears; select `distance` <=. When another box appears, select `other` and type `1.5`, then click on the `OK` button.

The next few steps must write the rest of the Alice instructions following the object behavior specified in the pseudocode. These instructions are almost the same as Alice instructions implemented in previous sections.

Figure 11.6 shows the complete implementation for the behavior of object `humvee` using the **If/Else** statement. To test the actual behavior of the object in Alice, click the `Play` button in the upper-left side of the Alice interface. The actual minimum value was set to 0.5 and the maximum value was set to 2.5 for the random values of the variable `distance`.

11.5 Repetition

The repetition control structure repeats a set of actions several times. In this control structure, also called a loop, either a counter or a specified condition determines the number of times the group of actions or operations will be performed. This group of actions is called a *repetition group*.

Most programming languages include three variations of the repetition control structure:

1. `for` loop
2. `while` loop
3. `repeat-until` loop

The `while` loop is the most general one. The other two repetition constructs can be expressed with the `while` loop.

Repetition with the `for` Loop

The `for` loop is useful when the number of times that the loop is carried out is known in advance. The `for` loop explicitly deals with a loop counter. For example, consider that the instructions of an action block are to be performed `N` times. If the value of `N` is `20`, the loop counter will have an initial value of `1` and a final value of `20`.

In a flowchart, the assignment of an initial value to a counter variable is indicated within a rectangular box above the loop. For every execution of the loop, the value of the counter variable is decremented in addition to the execution of the instructions in `Block1`. Figure 11.7 shows the flowchart of this loop.

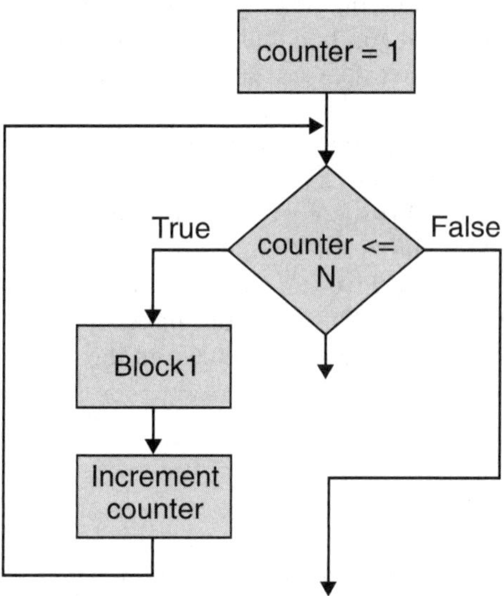

Figure 11.7 *Flowchart with a* `for` *loop.*

Using pseudocode, the `loop` statement is used to construct this type of loop. Sometimes, a `for` statement is used with the initial value and the final value of the loop counter.

The general structure of the `loop` statement in pseudocode follows. The repeat group consists of the instructions in `Block1`.

```
loop ⟨counter⟩ times
   do
      Block1
endloop
```

With every passage through the loop, the actions in `Block1` are executed and the loop counter is automatically incremented. The last time through the loop, the loop counter has its final value allowed. In other words, when the loop counter reaches its final value, the loop terminates. For example, assume that the `humvee` object is to perform a sequence of actions five times. The following pseudocode accomplishes this:

```
Move forward 1 meter
loop 5 times do
    Perform the following steps in simultaneously
        Turn right 0.2 revolutions
        Move forward 1.5 meters
endloop
Move forward 2.5 meters
```

Using Loops in Alice

The following sequence can be performed to use loops in Alice. Drag the tile of `Loop` control statement, located in the bottom of the `Editor` area (as shown in Figure 11.5), to the appropriate line of Alice code. An option box appears; select `5 times`. Construct the code statements for the instructions that are to be repeated and place them under the `loop` statement.

Figure 11.8 shows the Alice code with the simple loop statement that implements the behavior of object `humvee`. To test the implementation of the behavior of the object `humvee`, click on the `Play` button located on the upper-left corner of the Alice interface. The object starts to move to the left, then it take five turns and finally continues moving to the left.

The `while` Loop

With the `while` loop construct, the loop condition is tested first. If the condition is true, the actions in the repeat group are carried out. This continues until the condition evaluates to false. This type of loop is also called a pre-test loop because the condition is evaluated before the actions are performed.

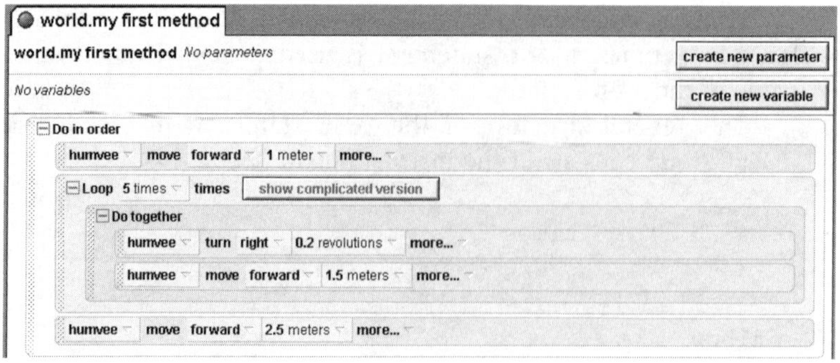

Figure 11.8 `Editor` *area with a simple loop in Alice.*

Figure 11.9 shows the repetition control structure, known as a `while` loop. The actions in `Block1` are repeated while the condition is true. This continues until the condition changes to false and the loop terminates. The control flow then continues with the actions that follow the `while` loop construct.

With pseudocode, the `while` statement is usually written with the keywords **while**, **do**, and **endwhile**. The repeat group consists of all actions in `Block1`, which is placed after the **do** keyword and before the **endwhile** keyword. The following portion of pseudocode shows the general structure for the `while` loop construct shown that corresponds to the portion of flowchart in Figure 11.9.

```
while ⟨condition⟩ do
   ⟨Block1⟩
endwhile
```

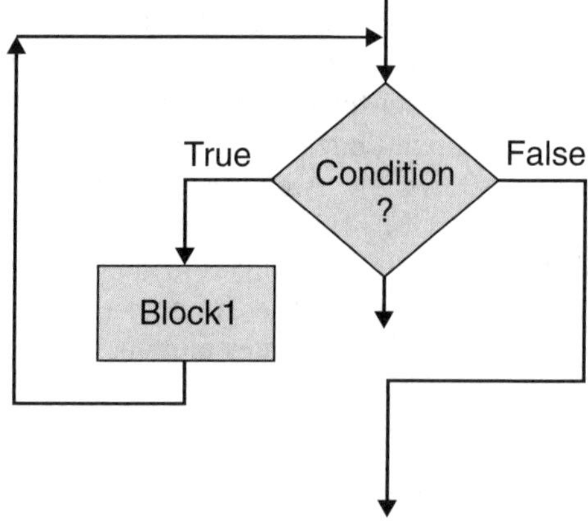

Figure 11.9 *A flowchart with a* `while` *loop control structure.*

Using while Loops in Alice

To simplify the application of a while loop in Alice, consider again the movement of object humvee. A variable distance will be used that takes a random value between 0.2 and 3.5, as in the previous example. The following pseudocode describes the object behavior:

```
Set distance to a random value between 0.2 and 3.5
Move forward for the random value in the distance variable
While distance <= 6.5 do
    Perform the following steps in simultaneously
        Turn right 0.2 revolutions
        Move forward 1.5 meters
    Set distance to distance + 1.5
endloop
Move forward 2.5 meters
```

To implement the description given in pseudocode for object humvee in Alice, follow the steps that were explained in the previous two examples. The main difference is the use of the while control statement.

Create variable distance as in the previous examples. Set a range of random values to the variable. Include the instruction for moving the humvee forward the value in the variable distance. For this, drag the tile of method move and drop it at the next line of code. An option box appears; select forward, then select expression and distance.

The next step is the construction of the line of code with the while statement. Drag the tile of the while control statement located at the bottom of the Editor area to the appropriate line of code. An option box appears; click true. Next drag the tile of variable distance and drop it on top of the tile with the true value of the while statement. An option box appears; select distance <=, then select other and type 6.5.

Figure 11.10 shows the Alice code with the implementation of the behavior of object humvee using the while control statement. To test this Alice program, click on the Play button and view the animation of the Alice world.

The repeat-until Loop

The construct for the repeat-until loop is similar to the while loop. In the repeat-until loop, the condition is evaluated after the repeat group. This means that the actions in the repeat group, Block1, will be performed until the condition is true. Figure 11.11 shows a portion of the flowchart for the loop-until construct. The actions in the loop will be carried out at least once.

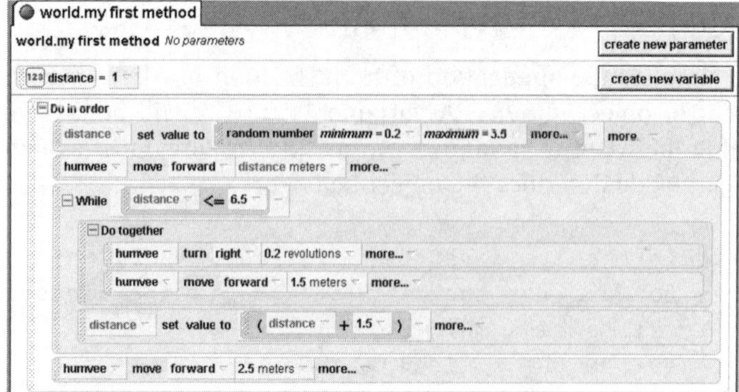

Figure 11.10 *Alice code with the* `while` *loop control structure.*

If the condition is true, the actions in the repeat group (`Block1`) will be performed only once.

The pseudocode for the `loop-until` construct is written with the `repeat` statement, which uses the keywords **repeat**, **until**, and **endrepeat**. Alice has no support for this loop construct but it can be implemented using the `while` statement. The repeat group consists of all actions after the **repeat** keyword and before the **until** keyword:

```
repeat
   ⟨Block1⟩
until ⟨condition⟩
endrepeat
```

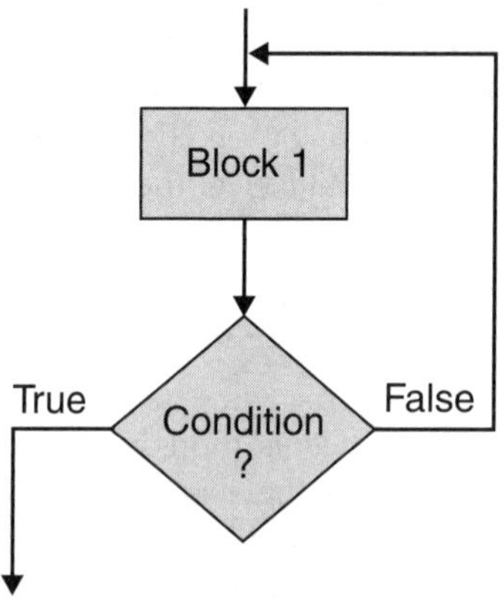

Figure 11.11 *Flowchart with a* `repeat-until` *loop control structure.*

Compilation is the task of translating a program from its source language to an equivalent program in binary code (possibly machine language). When the program executes in a computer, it reads the input data, carries out some computations, and writes the output data (results). A program is designed by using several control structures: sequence, selection, repetition, and input/output. The corresponding language statements are called control statements.

This manual has briefly explained how to develop programs in Alice, and it has shown the main features of the Alice system and how to construct simple programs. Several examples have illustrated how to do this.

Key Terms

Algorithm
Attributes
Byte-code
C++
Class
Compilation
Control statements
`Editor` area
Flowcharts
Functions
Instructions
Java
JVM
Loops
Methods
Object
Object tree
Program
Program execution
Programming language
Properties
Pseudo-code
Selection
Source code
Type
Variables
World

1. Explain the relevance of an Alice world. Give examples.
2. List and explain the various forms of object behavior that can be defined in Alice.
3. What is the difference between a class and an object? Explain with an example.
4. What are the differences between the properties and the behavior of objects? Give examples.
5. Explain the similarities and differences between sequential and simultaneous actions.
6. What is a programming language? Why do we need one? Why are there so many programming languages?
7. Explain the purpose of compilation. How many compilers are necessary for a given application? What is the difference between program compilation and program execution? Explain.
8. What is the real purpose of developing a program? Can we just use a spreadsheet program such as MS Excel to solve numerical problems? Explain.
9. Change one of the examples presented and give a more complete behavior of object `humvee`. The behavior should take much more time than any of the examples mentioned.
10. Construct an Alice program similar to the examples presented and provide behavior of object `humvee` that will include sequence, selection, and repletion in the same program. The animation in Alice should take much more time than any of the examples mentioned.
11. Construct an Alice program similar to the previous problem above with two objects of class `Humvee`. Include behavior of the objects with sequence, selection, and repletion in the same program. The animation should take much more time than any of the examples mentioned.

index